BEFORE THE HARVEST

LORRAINE BAILEY

First Printing, 2024
Digital: ISBN 978-1-0686676-1-9
Paperback: ISBN 978-1-0686676-2-6

For more information, contact:
lorraine@kingdomnetwork.ch
www.foodstorycollection.com

Contents

Chapter	v
INTRODUCTION	1
1 HARVESTS	5
2 FRUITS OF THE EARTH	9
3 THE ENEMY	15
4 THE FRUITS ROT	25
5 THE SOLUTION	33
6 SALVATION	39
7 BEFORE THE HARVEST	45
8 THE FINAL HARVEST	49
Notes	61
About the Author	62
Acknowledgements	63

INTRODUCTION

I have a package to share with you...

Its contents point the way to treasure hidden in plain sight. Like a parcel that leaves the warehouse in good condition, this package may arrive at your door a little scuffed, but its contents are precious. Before getting started, here are some facts to remember.

The size of the observable universe is 94 billion light years across, and 95% of it is a complete mystery. There are other universes about which we know nothing, and there is an 80-90% gap in our knowledge of what's in the ocean. Many pieces of the puzzle are yet to be found, but some people have still tried to build a picture. Today, many scientific theories remain theories but are creatively sold to the world as truth. Nothing in scientific theory is ever 100% sure because of human error, bias, and limitations in measuring tools and variables. Plenty of things scientists thought they knew 70 years ago were proven wrong. One thing is certain: there are unseen factors which affect us daily that science cannot answer, and there is still much to learn and understand.

In the meantime, while we wait for the scientific community to find funding to carry out further research, the earth is not waiting; it is maturing and moving towards something so significant that it will affect every living thing on this earth. Do you sense it? Have you ever thought something was not quite right in this world and that it was out of order? Many of us will not investigate further since we have no time to learn what we need to build a picture and come to an unbiased conclusion with 100% accuracy.

However, I must share a piece of treasured knowledge with you before the great harvest comes. As sure as the sun rises, a harvest is coming.

The content of this package is from someone who loves you more than you know. His followers know they will be misunderstood and persecuted for warning people and telling them the truth, but they do it anyway out of love.

We know from history that there truly was (*and is, and is to come*) a man named Jesus, and he was crucified on a cross for proclaiming to be the Son of God. The sign which hung over his cross read 'King of the Jews' as the reason he was being crucified. There were two criminals on the cross, dying next to Jesus, who also had signs of why they were being crucified. One of the criminals, although guilty and dying, followed the crowd in mocking and scoffing at Jesus. In contrast, the other criminal, who recognised his own dying state and diabolical situation, admitted he was a criminal and believed the **sign** that Jesus was his King. He also perceived that something was not quite right. The situation was out of order. Mockery and hate aimed at Jesus, who committed no crime and did no wrong. Why were so many misusing his name? Did they even know Jesus personally? Instead of following the crowd, he said to Jesus, 'Please remember me when you reach your kingdom.' Jesus responded with a promise that they would be together in paradise—a reward for his **uncowardly**, logical, and righteous perception of the situation.

'Before the Harvest' uses farming and technology analogies and metaphors to expose the problems on this earth. Once we understand who we are as humans and know the problem, the solution will be so clear that we have already used it in other scenarios with the same problem.

Imagine you are a landowner on this earth waiting for your fruits to ripen (the harvest). Within this analogical discourse, humans are like plants growing fruits on the earth, and the Creator is the landowner. A good fruit harvest is the end goal for the landowner who loves and cares for his plants, but the growing fruits become rotten, with some fruits not growing at all due to an enemy. After some investigation, the reason for the problem becomes clear (e.g., pests, viruses, trauma, land mismanagement), and the landowner provides one simple solution to save his plants from bearing rotten fruit before the harvest (anti-pest and anti-virus solutions, healing from trauma and better land management).

Like a crop cycle, humans have a beginning and an end, and the part in between—called life—is an opportunity to prepare before the final harvest of the world. If you were the plant growing in a quiet field, would you want to know that there will be a great harvest one day? Or **would you rather be unprepared and without knowledge?** This is sobering content, but so is eight years of reading the content of medical books to save lives. It's worth knowing because your life is worth saving.

Take heed. Many are drunk with deception, which has been force-fed into society. It takes bravery to exercise a righteous perception like the man next to Jesus on the cross who did not follow the crowd in their slander and mockery of an innocent man. Many individuals, corporations, and regimes reject the truth and do not want your problems fixed because they benefit from other people's weaknesses and ignorance. It is the truth that will set people free.

The solution explained in this discourse will offer great hope. It is not a philosophy, a religious rite, a man-made tradition, or a complicated ritual. It is simple and logical.

Before reading the contents, my request to you, beloved reader, is that you have ears willing to hear, an open heart, and an open mind toward the information I am eager to share with you.

"He who has ears to hear, let him hear."
(Matthew 13:9)

1

HARVESTS

"*While the earth remains, Seedtime and harvest, Cold and heat, Winter and summer, And day and night Shall not cease.*" (Genesis 8:22)

peangdao from Getty Images Pro

A crop growing fruits may look fine on the outside, but once you collect, open, or use them, the state of the fruit will be evident. The reasons for its bad or good state will take some investigation, but we all want the good and beneficial ones. All good landowners desire a good crop.

In today's digital age, the convenience of buying food products from supermarkets all year round has led to a generation that may need to remember to consider times, seasons, sowing, and reaping. Our knowledge of technology and digitalisation has grown, but our understanding of survival, i.e., managing the ground to grow food to eat, plants to create essentials and using wood to build our homes, is fading away. The bubble of convenience and the flood of distractions competing for our attention is enormous. One day, it will burst.

Here are a few reminders about farming and harvests:

1. Landowners (and farmers) sow seeds and hope for a harvest of good fruits at the end of the season. These fruits will be used or stored for good purposes.

2. During a harvest, farmers and hired workers collect, sort and clean mature or ripened crops. By the end of a good harvesting season, many traditionally celebrate their abundant crop with feasts and festivals! *"This is what the kingdom of God is like. A man scatters seed on the ground. Night and day, whether he sleeps or gets up, the seed sprouts and grows, though he does not know how. All by itself the soil produces grain —first the stalk, then the head, then the full kernel in the head. As soon as the grain is ripe, he puts the sickle to it, because the harvest has come."* (Mark 4:26-29).

3. There are various threats to a healthy crop. Crop failure may occur due to plant viruses/diseases, pests, land (earth) mismanagement, and environmental trauma, which can significantly diminish crop yield.

4. Good plants producing good fruit that survive these threats will be saved. Rotten fruits growing from a plant with a plant virus will be burned in a fire and destroyed.

"A farmer went out to sow his seed. As he was scattering the seed, some fell along the path, and the birds came and ate it up. Some fell on rocky places, where it did not have much soil. It sprang up quickly, because the soil was shallow. But when the sun came up, the plants were scorched, and they withered because they had no root. Other seed fell among thorns, which grew up and choked the plants. Still other seed fell on good soil, where it produced a crop—a hundred, sixty or thirty times what was sown. Whoever has ears, let them hear." (Matthew 13:1-23).

"He who sows the good seed is the Son of Man. The field is the world, the good seeds are the sons of the kingdom, but the tares are the sons of the wicked one. The enemy who sowed them is the devil, the harvest is the end of the age, and the reapers are the angels. Therefore as the tares are gathered and burned in the fire, so will it be at the end of this age. The Son of Man will send out His angels, and they will gather out of His kingdom all things that offend, and those who practice lawlessness, and will cast them into the furnace of fire. There will be wailing and gnashing of teeth. Then the righteous will shine forth as the sun in the kingdom of their Father. He who has ears to hear, let him hear!" (Matthew 13:37).

2

FRUITS OF THE EARTH

There are many different kinds of seeds, but they all have one thing in common: They produce fruit when planted in fertile earth.

pixelshot

In the beginning

1. The Creator said, "Let us make man in our own image." The Word spoken by the Creator was his seed.

2. The seed fell on the fertile earth, and the earth birthed mankind's physical/**visible human form**.

3. The visible human form comprises 99% of the earth's elements from which it came. i.e. Oxygen, hydrogen, nitrogen, carbon, calcium, phosphorus, sulfur, potassium, sodium, chlorine, and magnesium. When life leaves the physical body, those elements will return to the earth with the appearance of dust particles.
"Till you return to the ground, For out of it you were taken; For dust you are, And to dust you shall return." (Genesis 3:19).

4. The **invisible human form** (the soul) comprises a personality, emotions, and intelligence. Characteristics of the human soul can only be seen when manifesting those inner attributes. The soul comes from the unseen Creator. *"And the LORD God formed man of the dust of the ground, and breathed into his nostrils the breath of life, and man became a **living soul**"* (Genesis 2:7).

5. The name of the first children of the earth was Adam אָדָם, which means 'earth/ground, red/blood', which describes his physical form.

It starts with a thought

Human life began as a seed 'sown' in the earth. A father sowed the seed, and a mother birthed the child. The action of sowing a seed started as a thought in the mind. Thoughts are unseen unless we act on them or say them. If I think about growing an apple tree, you will never know unless I act on it and plant a seed. After I planted an apple seed, only witnesses who were there at the time would know I had done it. A witness may have written a record of the truth somewhere, but meanwhile, it remains a mystery to some.

Ten years later, when you consume my delicious apples, you may have no idea how the tree got there or that it belongs to me, especially if **I am 'unseen'**, i.e., travelling for a very long time. Logic will conclude that someone sowed an apple seed to grow an apple tree.

If an investigator **does not believe the seed sower exists** because they are unseen, then human error and bias would form the foundation of that scientific investigation with flawed scientific theories. Meanwhile, many enjoy the benefits of this earth without knowing where it came from or who sowed the seed.

If I am thinking of baking a cake, one would never know unless I say it or act on it. If I believe I can make a cake, I will step out in faith and make it. First, I would find the right natural ingredients, precisely measure them, mix them together, and then bake it at the right temperature for all to enjoy. The cake is now the physical manifestation of my thoughts. If you were not around when I made the cake, you might wonder who made it. If you really wanted to know who the baker is, you could investigate, including reading written accounts from witnesses. Logic would not assume the cake (the effect) made itself or just appeared on its own. The precision, the thought, and the skill behind its physical manifestation are the logical evidence required to conclude that someone made it. Believing I do not exist just because one cannot see me will block open thinking, skew opinion, and add limitations to research, leading to human bias.

Evolution: Did the cake I baked evolve from a scone? **No.** I used similar natural ingredients, techniques, and measurements to make both creations. The cake mixture itself evolved in the oven whilst transforming from a soupy liquid form to a solid form, but it was always a cake. You did not see me bake it, but it took thought and time to make it. Other bakers, makers, and creators often leave their mark on what they create, and those who have an eye for detail will identify when two separate creations belong to the same creator. DNA codes in humans and animals are very similar for this exact same reason. Computer programmers tend to reuse similar codes when building programs.

The oven used to bake both the cake and the scone did not bang its way into existence by itself. Someone skilled and intelligent carefully assembled the parts together and banged on parts for them to fit nicely. The Creator's words led to the physical manifestation of a perfect environment for mankind to grow and thrive with plants, trees, animals, water, sun, moon, and wind. From the Earth's perspective, it took a long time to grow and develop into the suitable conditions it has for us today. *But, beloved, do not forget this one thing: with the Lord, one day is as a thousand years, and a thousand years as one day (2 Peter 3:8).* The Creator is not limited to the earth's concept of time. Time in space is different to time on Earth. Six days in heaven is not six days on earth.

Humans of the earth

The Creator sowed a seed (through his Word). The word 'Seed' can be defined as the beginning or cause of something. When Jesus explained the 'parable of the sower' to his disciples, he said, *"Now the parable is this: The seed is the word of God"* (Luke 8:11). Adam came out of the earth. DNA-coded and in the likeness of his Father, Adam was also equipped with seeds to produce children and an intelligence to create. Everything was initially good. The plants were good. Mankind was good.

Then God said, "Let Us make man in Our image, according to Our likeness; let them have dominion over the fish of the sea, over the birds of the air, and over the cattle, over all the earth and over every creeping thing that creeps on the earth." So God created man in His own image; in the image of God He created him; male and female He created them. Then God blessed them, and God said to them, "Be fruitful and multiply; fill the earth and subdue it; have dominion over the fish of the sea, over the birds of the air, and over every living thing that moves on the earth."

And God said, "See, I have given you every herb that yields seed which is on the face of all the earth, and every tree whose fruit yields seed; to you it shall be for food. Also, to every beast of the earth, to every bird of the air, and to everything that creeps on the earth, in which there is life, I have given every green herb for food" and it was so. Then God saw everything that He had made, and indeed it was very good. So the evening and the morning were the sixth day. (Genesis 1: 26-31).

3

THE ENEMY

The variety of creatures that exist in the sky, ocean, and earth is substantial, and not all can be seen with the naked eye nor have they been discovered yet. The Creator created other living intelligent celestial beings outside the earth for different purposes and functions.

The Fall

"How you are fallen from heaven, O Lucifer, son of the morning! How you are cut down to the ground. You who weakened the nations! For you have said in your heart: 'I will ascend into heaven, I will exalt my throne above the stars of God; I will also sit on the mount of the congregation on the farthest sides of the north; I will ascend above the heights of the clouds, I will be like the Most High.' (Isaiah 14:12-14).

The great dragon was cast out, that serpent of old, called the Devil and Satan, who deceives the whole world; he was cast to the earth, and his angels were cast out with him (Revelation 12:9).

1. Fallen celestial beings who were once angels (messengers) of the Creator separated themselves from their original function and purpose. These fallen celestial beings are enemies of the Creator and everything the Creator loves. Unlike humans who have been given grace, these fallen beings have no opportunity for repentance or to be forgiven for treason.

2. These fallen angels are in a pure evil state of envy and hatred and are out to steal, kill, and destroy humans (John 10:10). The messages they give are wrong and are otherwise known as temptations. They send frequencies to the human host as messages or ideas to get you to believe and receive them. Once their messages are sown into your thoughts, they may manifest into actions/behaviours. That action devastates the human host directly or those around them.

3. These beings tempted the first humans and succeeded. An enemy hacked into the loving, pure, and peaceful state of mind and environment humans once had.

Seed of the serpent

Parasites wait for an entry point into your house/body (via a weak point or an open door). Once inside, they steal from you, and if you give it a chance, they would suck up the life from you. The more you feed it, the stronger it will get, but the sad thing is many do not realise they have a parasite. Like a parasite, there are evil forces at work against mankind.

"Now it came to pass, when men began to multiply on the face of the earth, and daughters were born to them, that the sons of God saw

the daughters of men, that they were beautiful; and they took wives for themselves of all whom they chose. (Genesis 6:1-2). There were giants on the earth in those days, and afterwards, when the sons of God came into the daughters of men, they bore children to them. Those were the mighty men who were of old, men of renown." (Genesis 6:4).

1. Ancient stories from civilisations worldwide say there were 'beings' (many called them 'gods') who came down to earth and had children with mortal women. The ideology, names, and details differed between the cultures that shared this story because the cultures and languages differed, but they fundamentally came from some element of truth. The bible says, *"And God looked upon the earth, and, behold, it was corrupt; for all flesh had corrupted his way upon the earth"* (Genesis 6:12). These giants/Nephilim were hybrid beings, i.e., both human and celestial beings. The flesh of some other creatures was also corrupted (DNA corruption) and needed to be wiped out. Nephilim were famous for achieving success on the earth and were worshipped and honoured as deities long after they died—even today in some religions. Like their fallen fathers (fallen celestial beings), they were corrupted and evil, doing the opposite of what the Creator intended.

2. When the Nephilim died in the flood, their flesh (physical state) died, but their unseen, unclean spirit remained on the earth where they were born. These are the children of the fallen beings and are the actual seed of the enemy. *So the LORD God said to the serpent* (Genesis 3:14). *I will put enmity between you and the woman, And between your seed and her Seed* (Genesis 3:14).

3. Jesus said...*"The kingdom of heaven is like a man who sowed good seed in his field. But while everyone was sleeping, his enemy came and sowed weeds among the wheat, and went away. When the wheat sprouted and formed heads, then the weeds also appeared. The owner's servants came to him and said, 'Sir, didn't you sow good seed in your field? Where then did the weeds come from?' 'An enemy did this,' he replied. The servants asked him, 'Do you want us to go and pull them up?' 'No,' he answered, 'because while you are pulling the weeds, you may uproot the wheat with them. Let both grow together until the harvest. At that time I will tell the harvesters: First collect the weeds and tie them in bundles to be burned; then gather the wheat and bring it into my barn.'"* (Matthew 13:24-30).

The Kingdom of Darkness (network of wickedness)

1. The kingdom of darkness is an organised network of fallen celestial beings, their seed/children (unclean spirits and demons), and the human vessels they inhabit or influence (Judas Iscariot. *"Then Satan entered Judas"* (Luke 22:3)).
2. Fallen celestial beings send messages/signals to the human vessel. If the human vessel eventually believes in and then acts on that message, unclean spirits/demons may have the legal right to enter.

   When inside the human host, they may oppress, attack, torment, depress, confuse and persecute the host and influence the human and their offspring to hurt, kill, rape, destroy, pervert, abuse, and rebel against the loving and good order the Creator has laid out for humans. The Creator provided a solution for this issue, which is good news.

3. Unfortunately, the kingdom of darkness has targeted human vessels with influence, fame, money and power to ruin lives because they have a larger impact, i.e., more people will get hurt under their influence. Jesus told certain influential religious people who were out to kill him, *"You are of your father the devil, and the desires of your father you want to do* (John 8:44). They aim to live their lives through a human vessel—like a parasite or a hacker.

4. Some humans knowingly work for the kingdom of darkness. There exist elite groups that want to maintain control or make money through your weaknesses, insecurities, illness, ignorance, and addictions and do not want you to be saved. How will they stay in power and make money if you are set free? Also, some humans knowingly invite unclean spirits into their bodies via witchcraft, sorcery and wizardry, and these are widely practiced today.

5. The kingdom of darkness has temporarily conquered many worldly systems by pushing certain ideologies and politics through the humans they work through. They are anti-salvation/Christ, anti-life, anti-human DNA, and against the order and plan of the Creator (See Table 1). Institutions working against the Creator's plan are a kingdom of darkness initiative. The Creator wants to save and give life, but the Kingdom of Darkness wants to destroy and kill.

6. Jesus cast out unclean spirits and demons **from humans** who were out on the streets, in their homes and **even in the synagogue/church.**

Now, there was a man in their synagogue with an unclean spirit. And he cried out, saying, "Let us alone! What have we to do with You, Jesus of Nazareth? Did You come to destroy us? I know who You are—the Holy

One of God!" But Jesus rebuked him, saying, "Be quiet, and come out of him!" And when the unclean spirit had convulsed him and cried out with a loud voice, he came out of him (Mark 1:23-26).

An Analogy

When one opens the window of a house, flies and pests can enter uninvited. In the same way, a computer hacker may gain access through trickery, if you click on the wrong button or link. If we open the door to hackers, they might enter and corrupt the system, regardless of whether you know the creator of that computer or not. Regardless of whether you think you are a good person or not and regardless of what title one carries, e.g. teacher, lawyer, Christian, president, priest, pastor, mother, father, politician, elite, rich, poor, powerful. Makes no difference.

Pray for wisdom, forgiveness, and grace! Parasites, hackers, and pests do not want to come out and want to live life through the physical human. The fungi Ophiocordyceps unilateralis (Zombie-ant fungus) is a loose example of that. Unclean spirits do not want to come out, but **they do not own** humans. The Creator sent the solution. Salvation came to free us and give us life, inner peace, love, joy, and real life.

Time-Out

Are you concerned about unclean spirits? Tell the Creator your concerns. He is your Father, and he loves you. He wants you to know you have an enemy and does not want you to be ignorant or to live in fear. Give Him any fears and worries you may have.

Fear not, for I am with you; Be not dismayed, for I am your God. I will strengthen you, Yes, I will help you, I will uphold you with My righteous right hand.'
(Isaiah 41:10)

If you want to be free, find Jesus or his real followers to help you. Read the scriptures yourself to avoid the pests coming in through a place you were unaware of. Gain knowledge, avoid ignorance. If you don't know Jesus personally and are unsure if you are a true follower, wait to read 'The Solution' and 'Salvation' described in chapters 5 & 6. Ask the Father to set you free and ask for wisdom to close any window in your life which you may have left open to pests.

"When an unclean spirit goes out of a man, he goes through dry places, seeking rest, and finds none. Then he says, 'I will return to my house from which I came.' And when he comes, he finds it empty, swept, and put in order. Then he goes and takes with him seven other spirits more wicked than himself, and they enter and dwell there; and the last state of that man is worse than the first. So shall it also be with this wicked generation." (Matthew 12:43-45).

The Anti-Christ

Table 1) Example of anti-Christ behaviour

Their aim	Strategy

Convince humans to believe a lie	• Offer religion without true salvation. • Mock and slander the saviour Jesus and ridicule or hate Jesus/his followers because of a lie told about him and his followers. (e.g. Nero Julius Caesar killed innocent Christians and had an anti-Christ spirit working through him). • Offer unbelief, appearing to be intelligent, scientific, politically correct and more acceptable in society.
Offer humans a fake saviour	• Deceive humans into formulating their own assumptions about a saviour instead of knowing or following the real and actual Christ, e.g. a cult. • Self-worship / idol worship (belief you can save yourself).
Destroy the opportunity for human salvation	• Convince the world there is no salvation. • Create legislation/policy that is anti-bible, anti-Christ • Corrupt human flesh / DNA code/ corruption of what makes us human. Only humans can be saved.

Dearly beloved, remember...

Fear not, for I am with you; Be not dismayed, for I am your God. I will strengthen you, Yes, I will help you, I will uphold you with My righteous right hand. (Isaiah 41:10).

I sought the Lord, and he answered me and delivered me from all my fears. (Psalm 34:4).

$$4$$

THE FRUITS ROT

The enemy tempts humans to 'miss the mark' from being like their Father, the Creator. The word used for missing the mark is sin. Being tempted to sin does not mean you have sinned. In the same way, being offered to participate in a robbery does not mean that you agree to it or will do it. Sin is when the thoughts agree with the temptation to do wrong, which becomes 'stinking thinking'. Once believed, the evil idea might be nurtured towards maturity. The final expression of sinful thinking manifests itself through behaviour, words, and actions. There was a thought process before the action.

Humans have been seduced into sin because evil is the nature of the unclean spirits, demons and fallen angels, which tempt us. Humanity's problem started when the first humans sinned. They disconnected themselves from the source of life.

An Analogy

When a computer is disconnected from its energy source, it's only a matter of time before it dies. During its life span, the computer may be used for noble purposes to function as it should. However, it may also become influenced by hackers and viruses.

When hackers and viruses affect a computer, it looks the same on the outside but no longer functions as it should unless it gets saved. If you own a corrupted computer, you might want to sell or get rid of it. However, the one who has spent thought and time to create it, knowing its true value, will want to save or fix it.

The rotting process

1. The Father told His children, *"**Don't eat** the fruit from the tree of the knowledge of good and evil; otherwise, you will surely die."* (Genesis 2:17).
2. The first humans did not take this warning seriously. **They disobeyed**.
3. A lying **voice** (an enemy) **enticed** Eve towards disobedience against her Father. The enticement was that disobeying would help her to be more like her Father, God whom she worshiped. That lying voice said words which slandered her Father and twisted the truth with a lie. The moment Eve believed the enticing voice was the moment doubt, insecurity and pride were sown in her thoughts, and it manifested when she ate the fruit. Her desire to be more like her Father by disobeying him was not logical, but the enticer had a way with words.
4. Disobedience opened the door for the enemy to disturb the human operating system. Humans no longer functioned in the good way they were made to function.

Do not be deceived, God is not mocked; for whatever a man sows, that he will also reap. For he who sows to his flesh will of the flesh reap cor-

ruption, but he who sows to the Spirit will of the Spirit reap everlasting life. (Galatians 6:7-8).

Missing the Mark / Sin

Table 2) Sin expressed through example confessions

Missing the mark	Example confessions of sin
Pride (in its many shades)	My tribe, my skin colour, my children, my education, and my intellect are better and above someone else's. Those people are below me in importance and I have no time for them. My knowledge or decisions cannot be wrong, I know better than others, and how dare someone like that challenge me. I need help, but will not accept help from others. I must be perfect at everything I do because I don't want them to think I am weak.
Lies	He lied to the police so that his friend could get away with crime.

Covet	I want her husband or her house, her things, her career *(I am ungrateful with what I have)*. I want what belongs to another *(I might even steal it!)*.
Jealously/Envy	I feel uncomfortable and unhappy because she has something that I should have. I feel resentful or angry because she does something I desire to do for myself.
Hate/Self-hatred	He said he hates himself and wants to cut his body and remove a healthy body part.
Killing	She ended the life of another human being living in her womb because that innocent life is not considered as killing in her culture. He killed a human life to make a tribal sacrifice, which is accepted in his native culture. The teacher killed him with her words. He's now given up on life.

Murder	He thought the school were to blame for his problems and wished they were all dead. He eventually took his gun and murdered innocent people there.
Bitterness/ Unforgiveness	He didn't forgive, which led to bitterness of heart and eventually ill health (mental and physical). She didn't forgive me when I apologized but I'm enjoying my life and have moved on. She is still angry.
Slander	She is making videos against another Christian man which may not be true (destroying his reputation and dejecting him).
Gossip	They spread rumours about her without the full picture and now they judge her and treat her poorly.
Adultery	He has sexual relations with a woman he is not married to or lustful thoughts of someone who is not his wife.
Blasphemy	He mocks the Creator. He tells everyone he is a god (to be worshiped) and uses the name of the Creator as a curse word or in vain talk.

Idol worship	He worships a man-made image he call's 'god' i.e. an image, self, a statue, a celebrity. They worship creation/nature instead of the Creator that made it. Money comes first in my life. I would do anything to get it.
Dis-honouring parents	I gave birth, fed, nurtured, forgave, loved, and taught my son, but now he refuses to help his elderly parents.
Sexual perversions (abuse, self-abuse, sexual relations outside the original design of mankind) Lusts of the flesh (drug abuse, greed, adultery)	Your garden was pure, but due to mismanagement or a crisis, a pest got in and messed it up, leaving chaos and residue which hinders good fruit from growing. The original purpose of the garden is to grow fruit, multiply and enjoy with one legally allowed to enter. Without having boundaries, many will disrespect, ruin and mistreat the garden. When that garden is mistreated, it may affect the other gardens nearby.
Stealing	I saw him take what he had no permission to take.

No sabbath day	Taking no day in the week to rest hurts the mind and body. (The maker of a machine turns the power off once a week to reboot and refresh the device so that it functions well.)
Witchcraft (rebellion, sorcery, wizardry, occult, new-age)	She used her knowledge of sorcery and witchcraft to achieve her selfish will which is for power and control.

Other ways we humans miss the mark

Hypocrisy – e.g., being hateful because someone else was hateful. Judging someone for being judgmental. Gossiping about someone who gossiped about you. Greed, fractions, strife, rage/anger. (Read Galatians 5:19-21 and Revelation 21:8).

We have not measured up. Those you think are perfect may have sinned against someone else. The Father can see everything, including what happens behind closed doors and our thoughts. However, we have a great living hope. We have a Father to whom we belong and who desires to bring repair, cleaning, and transformation to his children's hearts! He provided the solution.

We have all sinned

If we say that we have no sin, we deceive ourselves, and the truth is not in us (1 John 1:8). *For all have sinned and fall short of the glory of God.* (Romans 3:23).

Also He spoke this parable to some who trusted in themselves that they were righteous, and despised others:

"Two men went up to the temple to pray, one a Pharisee and the other a tax collector. The Pharisee stood and prayed thus with himself, 'God, I thank You that I am not like other men—extortioners, unjust, adulterers, or even as this tax collector. I fast twice a week; I give tithes of all that I possess.' And the tax collector, standing afar off, would not so much as raise his eyes to heaven, but beat his breast, saying, **'God, be merciful to me a sinner!'** *I tell you, this man went down to his house justified rather than the other; for everyone who exalts himself will be humbled, and he who humbles himself will be exalted."* (Luke 18:9-14)

My little children, these things I write to you, so that you may not sin. And if anyone sins, we have an Advocate with the Father, Jesus Christ the righteous. (1 John 2:1)

5

THE SOLUTION

*"For God so loved the world that He gave His only begotten Son, that whoever believes in Him **should not perish** but have everlasting life."* (John 3:16).

Analogy 1: Corrupted computer

Problem

The computer has many components, none of which were designed for corruption. When it has been corrupted by malware, i.e., viruses or hackers, it acts out of order and in ways it was not meant to act. The computer may not know its poor state, but the one who uses it will identify that something is wrong. Only the one who loves or owns it would care enough to provide a solution to fix it. Many could have thrown the corrupted one away and bought a new one, but not a loving owner who also knows the true value of that computer's content.

Solution

The human who owns and loves their corrupted computer cannot physically enter it to stop the violation. Therefore, the only solution must come in a format the computer can receive to 1) remove the virus, 2) cast out the hacker/s, 3) guard it against falling prey to enemies again, and 4) bring it to its original purpose. The solution for the computer is called anti-malware.

Analogy 2: Corrupted fruit

Problem

The plant from which the fruit grows was not intended to become rotten. Plants react poorly when plant viruses or diseases, insects/pests, poor land management, and natural disasters have corrupted them. The fruits growing from the plant will eventually display signs of rot; sometimes, the fruit looks normal outside, but there is rot deep inside the core.

The plant may not know its poor state, but the one who tastes and uses its fruit will identify that something is off. Only the landowner who loves the crop would care enough to provide a solution to fix it. Many could have destroyed the corrupt plants and started again, but not a loving landowner who knows the true value of the fruit.

Solution

The landowner loves the plants but cannot physically enter into the plant to stop the violation, virus, disease, or pests. Therefore, the only solution must come in a format the field of crops can receive, and that is to have good field workers looking after the crop to 1) give it what it needs to remove the viruses/diseases, 2) cast out the pest(s), 3) guard it against falling prey to enemies, and 4) bring it to its original purpose, giving plants what they need to thrive and grow good fruit.

Corrupted earth

Problem

Humans were not originally designed for corruption, sin, disease, unclean spirits, or demon possession. When we sinned, this gave the kingdom of darkness access to use, abuse and manipulate the earth.

So the great dragon was cast out, that serpent of old, called the Devil and Satan, who deceives the whole world; he was cast to the earth, and his angels were cast out with him. (Revelation 12:9). When someone sins against us, we say, 'That's out of order'. When the fruit of the earth rots, others can smell it, but some might ignore it because they think it's normal. Sin/'stinking thinking' may also cause the body to react from a cellular, epigenetic level, which is passed on from generation to generation and can manifest in the body and mind as illness and disease.

Solution

Only the one who created the earth and still loves it would care enough to provide a solution to fix it. Many by now would have destroyed the corrupted version and started again, but not a loving Creator who knows the true value of the earth and the good children it could produce.

The Creator Father, who loves and cares for the earth, needed to be able to enter the earth and fix it. Therefore, His solution was to come through His only begotten Son in human form, which the Earth could receive. The begotten Son is the perfect image of His Father. *When you see the Son, you have seen the Father* (John 14:9).

The only begotten Son is the Word/Seed from the Father, who contained incorruptible, holy DNA, sinless blood, which, when it poured out into the ground/earth (from which humans are from), a transaction was made. The blood of the Son of God purifies and sanctifies our corrupted, sinful state. The Son shed his blood, died and came alive again to 1) give humans what they need to be cleansed and overcome sin, 2) cast out unclean spirits and de-mon/s 3) guard them against falling prey to enemies, and 4) bring humans to their original purpose (giving humans what they need (*not want*) to thrive and grow good fruit). The name of the only begotten Son is Yeshua, which means salvation. *This is good news!*

Ground conditions

A farmer prepares the ground by loosening or raking the soil to receive the good seed. Humans whose hearts have been broken, humbled, worked on, and prepared have the best conditions for receiving the Seed (the Word/Yeshua). Once the seed is rooted, it will grow, and if it is watered and nurtured with regular rays of sunshine (being in the presence of the Son), that seed can grow into the size of a mustard tree. It's only a matter of time. The Word which took root will grow into something that will help and bless many.

Then He said, "What is the kingdom of God like? And to what shall I compare it? It is like a mustard seed, which a man took and put in his garden; and it grew and became a large tree, and the birds of the air nested in its branches." (Luke 13:18-19).

Accepting the solution

Before a computer downloads any anti-malware solution, the owner would have acknowledged that there is an issue and would have been willing to fix it. Before installing anti-malware, an agreement must be reached by clicking a 'yes' button in the pop-up window. This agreement starts the cleaning process and provides future protection against corruption, and it takes a moment to load. Depending on several factors, the moment of loading can take a very long time or seconds.

Humans have been offered the solution. If that person admits they have a problem and is willing to be helped, they can agree /say 'yes' to the solution. The solution is fully receiving Jesus in one's heart like a download (i.e. the seed in your ground/the Word in your heart).

And as they were eating, Jesus took bread, blessed and broke it, and gave it to the disciples and said, "Take, eat; this is My body." Then He took the cup, and gave thanks, and gave it to them, saying, "Drink from it, all of you. For this is My blood of the new covenant, which is shed for many for the remission of sins (Matthew 26:26-30). Depending on many factors, downloading might take a lifetime, years, or minutes.

Rejecting the solution

If the computer says 'no' and rejects the anti-malware solution, the operating system will continue to' act up' with bugs and potential hackers. Eventually, the computer may become overrun by other hackers and pulled away from its real purpose, and the original user cannot use it for good purposes. All corrupted computers that refuse to be saved from hackers and malware will be signposted as 'out of order' until the workers remove the damaged machines and throw them away. Occasionally, opportunities to fix the computer will be offered, but out of pride, it may still refuse.

The landowner wants to help his crop reach its full potential, so he cuts and prunes the field to increase the likelihood of good fruit growth.

For the wages of sin is death, but the **gift of God is eternal life in Christ Jesus our Lord.** (Romans 6:23). *Unless you repent you will all likewise perish* (Luke 13:3). *However, If we confess our sins, He is faithful and just to forgive us our sins and to cleanse us from all unrighteousness.* (1 John 1:9).

6

SALVATION

The Creator's solution came in a form we can receive. The solution is salvation, which is the meaning of Yeshua. Yeshua was translated to Iēsous in Greek and later to Jesus in English.

With corruption on earth and rot affecting humans' hearts, Jesus's death on the cross and his shed blood was the download the earth required for the clean-up process to begin. His flesh was broken, and his blood was shed, which ensured our corrupted blood and flesh would be atoned for and the rot gone in time for harvest.

Prophecies

Many foretold and prophesied in literature and ancient scriptures about the Anointed One coming to save mankind. There were also natural signs in the sky and visitations from prominent wisemen from different parts of the world. When salvation came in the humble human form of Yeshua, born in Bethlehem, he fit the description written in scripture, but he did not meet man-made expectations nor incorrect human interpretations upheld in stiff-necked human traditions. Many still rely on the opinions and interpretations of their leaders rather than read the truth or seek the Creator (the source of truth) for themselves. (Read Isaiah 53).

It's Personal

Hearing what others say will never be the same as a personal experience of getting to know someone. Researching the scriptures and hearing what witnesses say and write about Him is a good start. Some have had personal encounters, dreams, and visions or heard his words audibly, or through another human vessel or creation, or in His words (scripture), which resonated in their hearts. When it comes to Jesus, no words are good enough to describe how wonderful he is.

At 12 years of age, while alone in my room and on my knees, I encountered Yeshua of Nazareth. I heard His voice and beheld His beautiful light. Shortly after this, my grandma entered the room, completely unaware of my recent experience with the Saviour and asked me if I wanted to give my life to Jesus. She guided me in a simple sinner's prayer, and right there, in a small act of faith, I asked Jesus to come into my life, take away my sins, and save and lead me. I did not have much understanding, but I knew Jesus was real and wonderful. Why wouldn't I ask him to come into my life? I never told my grandma or anyone else of that encounter for many years of my life.

The four witness accounts already written about Jesus being the Saviour, Son of God, healer, deliverer, and teacher who was killed on the cross and then rose from the dead on the 3rd day didn't even cross my mind at that time because I had not read the bible. I was only 12 years old. My family did not go to church often.

I called on the name of the LORD at 12 years old, and He answered me in a specific way. I was a child, open, humbled by life's circumstances, poor in spirit, and a witness of a few healings, but this was not about religion at all. It was **all about having a relationship with our Father**, and I needed Yeshua to get back to Him because of my sins.

Blessed are the poor in spirit, for theirs is the kingdom of Heaven (Matthew 5:3–12).

*"But without faith it is impossible to please Him, for he who comes to God must believe that He is, and that He is a **rewarder of those who diligently seek Him**."* (Hebrews 11:6).

*For **"whoever calls on the name of the LORD shall be saved."*** (Romans 10:13-15).

"How then shall they call on Him in whom they have not believed? And how shall they believe in Him of whom they have not heard? And how shall they hear without a preacher? And how shall they preach unless they are sent? As it is written: 'How beautiful are the feet of those who preach the gospel of peace, Who bring glad tidings of good things!'" (Romans 10:13-15).

Jesus said...

'Repent', 'Believe the gospel' (Mark 1:15).

"Jesus said to him, 'I am the way, and the truth, and the life. No one comes to the Father except through me.'"
(John 14:6).

Jesus said to her, 'I am the resurrection and the life. Whoever believes in me, though he die, yet shall he live.'"
(John 11:25).

"For whoever desires to save his life will lose it, but whoever loses his life for My sake will find it"
(Matthew 16:25).

"You shall love the Lord your God with all your heart, with all your soul, and with all your mind.'
(Mathew 22:37).

"And the second is like it: Love your neighbour as yourself." (Mathew 22:39).

"This, then, is how you should pray: 'Our Father in heaven, hallowed be your name, your kingdom come, your will be done, on earth as it is in heaven. Give us today our daily bread. And forgive us our debts as we also have forgiven our debtors. And lead us not into temptation, but deliver us from the evil one." (Matthew 6:9-13).

Jesus Warns us

"It is better for you to enter into life maimed, rather than having two hands, to go to hell, into the fire that shall never be quenched where their worm does not die and the fire is not quenched." (Mark 9: 43-44).

"Then He will also say to those on the left hand, 'Depart from Me, you cursed, into the everlasting fire prepared for the devil and his angels.'" (Mathew 25:41).

Time Out:

Breathe for a minute and **talk to Jesus**, the Savior. Share what's on your heart. Reflect on his words.

Jesus speaks

Behold, I stand at the door and knock. If anyone hears My voice and opens the door, I will come into him and dine with him, and he with Me. (Revelation 3:20).

Getty Images

7

—————

BEFORE THE
HARVEST

A **summary of the events before the harvest:**

Stage 1: Earth and fruit corruption

- The landowner sowed seed on the earth, which became his children when His own beloved earth (which He designed Himself) birthed them, i.e., they were made out of the earth's element (read Chapter 2: Fruit of the Earth).
- The children picked up the 'virus' of sin from an enemy, which spread to their offspring, all with varying degrees of infection (Read Chapter 4: The Fruits Rot).
- The landowner's earth gradually became invaded by a network of wickedness (Read Chapter 3: The Enemy).

Stage 2: The Landowner's solution

- The landowner tried different techniques to fix the problem, often sending other workers to help good fruit grow

45

to its full potential, but this wasn't effective. Those workers were either killed or didn't love the field enough to take care of it. Many of the fruits which grew were artificially good.

- The Landowner knew the only way to fix the problem was to send His begotten Son into a hostile field which crushed, hurt and bruised him. The breaking of the Son's body and shedding of his blood opened up forgiveness of sin, healing and cleansing properties for the whole earth (Read Chapters 5 & 6: The Solution and Salvation). *"I am the living bread which came down from heaven. If anyone eats of this bread, he will live forever; and the bread that I shall give is My flesh, which I shall give for the life of the world."* (John 6:51).

Stage 3: The earth's response

- Some weak and humble humans who knew they were in bad condition received the solution and were transformed. They started to develop good character traits genuinely. (Read Chapter 8: The Final Harvest)
- Some did not receive the solution because they had shallow, hard, or distracted hearts, and others may not have known about it.

The problems are clear, and the Landowner has provided the solution. It is up to each individual who hears this good news to respond to that solution before the harvest.

Here is how we can prepare for salvation—the solution against the rot in time for harvest.

Table 3) Preparation before the harvest

For new plants	*For humans*
Loosen the soil and open the ground	Humble our heart and open it to receive.
Receive the good seed and allow it to take root	Receive the Word (Jesus) and allow the Word to take root.
Allow good farmers to protect and look after you	Allow the good shepherd, Jesus to protect and care for us directly and through his workers (angels, the saints, good parents, good pastors).
Grow good fruit without rot with regular pruning	Grow good character and keep a pure heart by letting the Word of God teach and wash us daily and by learning from life's lessons i.e. going through trials and tribulations and practicing gratefulness.
Stay connected to the vine with the other branches.	Remain connected to the Jesus (Read John 15:1-11). Build connections with his other followers. (Read Matthew 18:19-20).

The Kingdom of God

"The time is fulfilled, and the kingdom of God is at hand; repent and believe in the gospel." (Mark 1:15).

There are many kingdoms on this earth, and corruption can be found in most, if not all, worldly kingdoms. Greed, imbalanced scales, war, competition, and abuse of power from worldly leaders cause inhabitants grief, death, pain, hunger, and financial instability. World suffering results from sin and hearts that have not repented nor received the solution/salvation. The earth has been misused, abused, and disrespected, and so nature has reacted to the chaos of sin. The only Kingdom without corruption is one led purely by the Creator of Heaven and Earth through His Son, Yeshua / Jesus.

Two thousand years ago on earth, Jesus demonstrated the Kingdom of God with peace, love, joy, wholeness, goodness, patience, self-control, power, humility, generosity, and creativity. Jesus and His disciples, past and present, from all over the earth, demonstrate the Kingdom of God by freeing people from the effects of sin (through teaching, preaching, counselling, healing, delivering, and working miracles). *"These signs will follow those who truly believe."* (Mark 16:17-18).

8

===

THE FINAL HARVEST

*A*nd another angel came out of the temple, crying with a loud voice *to Him who sat on the cloud,* **"Thrust in Your sickle and reap, for the time has come** *for You to reap, for the* **harvest of the earth is ripe."** (Revelation 14:15).

Getty Images Signature

After a very long period of growth, the crops become ripe for picking. Crops grow peacefully on a field with minimal interference for a long time. But, when harvest time comes, there is a great commotion and a 'shaking' in the field with tractors and farmers pulling, collecting and sorting the good from the bad fruits.

The harvest is sudden, harsh, and extreme from the plant's point of view because, prior to that, not much was happening except for the occasional pest and environmental trauma.

Getty Images

The landowner will send his farmers to the field at an appointed time. Suddenly, the saved humans, i.e. those now with good hearts (no more rot by the grace of God), will be picked up during the final harvest, and the Son, Jesus, will meet them **in the air** (not from the ground) upon their collection (by the farmers/angels). This event will happen right after a terrible tribulation period on the earth.

The Great Tribulation

There will be great tribulation on this earth mid-way through a significant 7-year period before the harvest. Prophecies of old and of today warn us of diabolical events from Prophets who recorded what God had told them about the end of the age.

Many Christians bravely went through tribulation during the first, second, and third centuries, which ended during the 3rd century. They did not align with certain sinful man-made traditions or sin by worshiping Roman emperors Nero and Diocletian, who believed they were 'gods'. Under their prideful and boastful rule, Christians who were caught were killed in public and many went into hiding. Slander and lies were told about the followers of Jesus (who they named as 'Christians'), and unfortunately, the propaganda was believed by the public and used as a justification to kill Christians. **History will repeat itself** until the final harvest.

Apostle John saw a vision of end-time events and said of the beast: *And it was given unto him to **make war with the saints**, and to **overcome them**: and power was given him over all kindreds, and tongues, and nations. And all that dwell upon the earth shall worship him, whose names are not written in the book of life of the Lamb slain from the foundation of the world. If any man have an ear, let him hear. **He that leadeth into captivity shall go into captivity**: he that killeth with the sword must be killed with the sword. Here is the patience and the faith of the saints.* (Revelation 13:4-10).

Various beliefs exist about the end times through man-made expectations of an easy exit, possibly due to fear. As a result, scripture has been taken out of context to suit that narrative, but Jesus was clear (see Matthew 24:9-10). After witnesses display acts of God's power for three and a half years and are then killed, they will be risen up on the 'third day' and collected/saved in a one-time event before the devastation of the earth (bowls of God's wrath). (Read Revelation 16). Those who are still alive will be taken up (raptured) after those who were killed.

*And those of the people who understand shall instruct many; yet for many days they shall fall by sword and flame, by captivity and plundering. Now when they fall, **they shall be aided with a little help**; but **many shall join with them by intrigue**.* (Daniel 11:33-34).

Idol worship

And they worshiped the dragon which gave power unto the beast: and they worshiped the beast, saying, Who is like unto the beast? who is able to make war with him?

And there was given unto him a mouth speaking great things and blasphemies, and power was given unto him to continue forty and two months. And he opened his mouth in blasphemy against God, to blaspheme his name, and his tabernacle, and them that dwell in heaven. (Revelation 13:3-6).

With that said, we are not to fear the enemy nor follow the crowd. Many will follow out of fear and wonder. Many will not believe the warnings (due to believing fake news/slander and lies told against those in the know). **Do not get the mark of the Beast** and worship no image, idol, famous dictator or regime of this world nor show your allegiance towards it. Many will be coerced to get this mark and lives and/or livelihood will be threatened. Do not get the mark of the beast. (Read the book of Revelation 13 & 14).

The mark that the 'beast' or regime/king/kingdom will force people to get will be a corruption of the flesh (as it will be added to the right hand or forehead) and possibly a corruption of human DNA. The Mark of the Beast will be forced on people and may be sold under the pretense that it is for 'peace' and 'safety' reasons and/or possibly to 'upgrade' your 'humanness' or make you 'god-like'. Remember the lie the serpent told Eve in the garden?. Eating the fruit from the tree of the knowledge of good and evil did not make Eve 'more like God', it did the opposite, and her actions led her to be driven out of paradise. Lying words will entice many and therefore we follow no-one to receive this mark. Not even those with fame, a title of importance, a 'good' track record, or 'religious' status. **With this mark**, humans will be **irreversibly** rotted (Revelation 16:2), **cannot be saved** (Revelation 14:9-11) and will not make it home to heaven.

If I tried to return a MacBook to the Apple store which I re-coded and re-branded, it would not be accepted as a return item because it is no longer an original MacBook. It would be an abomination to the original maker. Humans were **originally** made in the image and likeness of our good Father God in heaven and a child's image of their father depends on their DNA code and similitude of character and personality.

The trials and tribulations believers experience as a result of not worshiping idols/getting the mark of the beast, will come with the Lords supernatural peace and strength to endure. The Landowners earth freely grows plants for eating and living. The children of Israel set up booths and tents during the wilderness at the time of the Exodus and so may it be near the end when some believers are in exile. The feast of booths will be commemorated for generations to come (Zechariah 14:16).

Because thou hast kept the word of my patience, I also will keep thee from the hour of temptation, which shall come upon all the world, to try them that dwell upon the earth. ***Behold, I come quickly:*** (Revelation 3:10-11). **Jesus the Christ**, Yeshua Ha-Mashiach, **will return, and all will see Him**.

Denying Jesus would be a grave error

Many will be offended and fall away from Christianity. Some because they believe the slander and fake news told against believers, some because they follow false leaders into doing so and some out of fear.

Two thousand years ago on earth, Jesus was being slandered against and was arrested as a result of lies and fake news about him. Peter kept in brief company with unbelievers who identified him as being a 'follower of Jesus' as though it were a bad thing. In response to fear of also being mistreated and potentially arrested, Peter denied he knew Jesus. He later repented.

"Now when they had kindled a fire in the midst of the courtyard and sat down together, Peter sat among them. And a certain servant girl, seeing him as he sat by the fire, looked intently at him and said, "This man was also with Him." But he denied Him, saying, "Woman, I do not know Him." And after a little while another saw him and said, "You also are of them." But Peter said, "Man, I am not!" Then after about an hour had passed, another confidently affirmed, saying, "Surely this fellow also was with Him, for he is a Galilean." But Peter said, "Man, I do not know what you are saying!" Immediately, while he was still speaking, the rooster crowed. And the Lord turned and looked at Peter. Then Peter remembered the word of the Lord, how He had said to him, "Before the rooster crows, you will deny Me three times." So Peter went out and wept bitterly. (Luke 22:55-62).

The offence may come from a misunderstanding in scripture or things not going as expected. Many religious people during Jesus' time misunderstood scripture or looked for scripture which suited their schedule or immediate need. Many wanted their Messiah (the Anointed One) to immediately eliminate their oppressors, the Romans, who were occupying the region at that time. When Jesus came, he didn't do what they wanted nor act or look the way they expected, and some were offended by that. Man-made traditions can become an idol.

.

Jesus said...

For then there will be great tribulation, such as has not been since the beginning of the world until this time, no, nor ever shall be. And unless those days were shortened, no flesh would be saved; but for the elect's sake those days will be shortened.

"Then if anyone says to you, 'Look, here is the Christ!' or 'There!' do not believe it. For false Christs and false prophets will rise and show great signs and wonders to deceive, if possible, even the elect. See, I have told you beforehand.

"Therefore if they say to you, 'Look, He is in the desert!' do not go out; or 'Look, He is in the inner rooms!' do not believe it. For as the lightning comes from the east and flashes to the west, so also will the coming of the Son of Man be. (Matthew 24:21-27).

"Immediately after the tribulation of those days the sun will be darkened, and the moon will not give its light; the stars will fall from heaven, and the powers of the heavens will be shaken. Then the sign of the Son of Man will appear in heaven, and then all the tribes of the earth will mourn, and they will see the Son of Man coming on the clouds of heaven with power and great glory. And He will send His angels with a great sound of a trumpet, and they will gather together His elect from the four winds, from one end of heaven to the other. (Matthew 24:29-31).

The Final Harvest, Jesus Returns & Judgement

"But of that day and hour no one knows, not even the angels of heaven, but My Father only. But as the days of Noah were, so also will the coming of the Son of Man be. For as in the days before the flood, they were eating and drinking, marrying and giving in marriage, until the day that Noah entered the ark, and did not know until the flood came and took them all away, so also will the coming of the Son of Man be. **Then two men will be in the field: one will be taken and the other left. Two women will be grinding at the mill: one will be taken and the other left.** *Watch therefore, for you do not know what hour your Lord is coming. But know this, that if the master of the house had known what hour the thief would come, he would have watched and not allowed*

his house to be broken into. **Therefore you also be ready, for the Son of Man is coming at an hour you do not expect.** (Matthew 24:36-44).

Jesus will return. *"I was watching in the night visions, And behold, One like the Son of Man, Coming with the clouds of heaven! He came to the Ancient of Days, And they brought Him near before Him. Then to Him was given dominion and glory and a kingdom, That all peoples, nations, and languages should serve Him. His dominion is an everlasting dominion, Which shall not pass away, And His kingdom the one Which shall not be destroyed.* (Daniel 7:13-14).

Therefore be patient, brethren, **until the coming of the Lord.** *See how* **the farmer waits for the precious fruit of the earth,** *waiting patiently for it until it receives the early and latter rain.* (James 5:7).

O Judah, **a harvest is appointed for you,** *When I return the captives of My people.* (Hosea 6:11).

For the **LORD is our Judge,** *The LORD is our Lawgiver, The LORD is our King; He will save us* (Isaiah 33:22).

Take Action

We have all sinned, fallen short of God's glory, and need salvation. (Romans 3:23).

When you pray, go into your room, and **when you have shut your door, pray to your Father** *who is in the secret place; and your Father who sees in secret* **will reward you** (Matthew 6:6).

Let's pray

Dear Heavenly Father, I praise you and bless Your holy name. Thank you for everything you have done and for offering me salvation. I receive and believe in Your Son, Jesus of Nazareth, who died on the cross to save me from my sins. He rose from the dead on the third day and is alive. His innocent blood was shed, and his body broken for me, which I take and receive.

Please forgive me of sin, as I also forgive all those who sinned against me. Cleanse my heart and mind and redeem me.

As I start (or re-start) a journey with You, please send me the help and counsel of the Holy Spirit so that I do Your will. I ask for a special blessing to have an abundant life in Christ and to endure the pruning seasons when life gets hard. Bless me with increased faith and trust that You are in full control.

Please put me in a blessed community with other believers and followers of Jesus. Save and redeem my family and friends, and help them know the truth and be saved as well.

In the name of my Saviour and Lord Jesus Christ.

Amen!

Likewise, I say to you, there is joy in the presence of the angels of God over one sinner who repents. (Luke 15:10)

Nuggets of wisdom

- **Read** the gospels yourself and with others to get to know the true God of heaven and earth.
- **Pray always**, including before reading the bible.

- **Ask, seek and learn** about the character of your Father and identify what's not of Him. Learn about God's promises for your life: *"My people are destroyed for lack of knowledge."* (Hosea 4:6). One day you will receive, you shall find, and the door will open (Matthew 7:7-8).

- Find a **bible teaching community of Christ followers** and avoid communities that worship human idols (cults) and who prioritise man-made traditions/culture (false religion).

- Have **faith and believe** *"that if you confess with your mouth the Lord Jesus and believe in your heart that God has raised Him from the dead, you will be saved."* (Romans 10:9).

- **Be humble.** *Then Jesus called a little child to Him, set him in the midst of them, and said, "Assuredly, I say to you, unless you are converted and become as little children, you will by no means enter the kingdom of heaven. Therefore whoever humbles himself as this little child is the greatest in the kingdom of heaven. Whoever receives one little child like this in My name receives Me* (Matthew 18:2-5). *"God resists the proud, but gives grace to the humble."* (James 4:6).

- **Take steps of faith**. Believe the good news and act on it (faith).

- **Hold on tightly to Jesus in all seasons** like a branch on a vine. Invite him into your home/temple/body.

Jesus says... *"I am the true vine, and My Father is the vinedresser. Every branch in Me that does not bear fruit He takes away; and every branch that bears fruit He prunes, that it may bear more fruit. You are already clean because of the word which I have spoken to you. Abide in Me, and I in you. As the branch cannot bear fruit of itself, unless it abides in the vine, neither can you, unless you abide in Me. "I am the vine, you are the branches. He who abides in Me, and I in him, bears much fruit; for without Me you can do nothing. If anyone does not abide in Me, he is cast out as a branch and is withered; and they gather them and throw them into the fire, and they are burned. If you abide in Me, and My words abide in you, you will ask what you desire, and it shall be done for you. By this My Father is glorified, that you bear much fruit; so you will be My disciples.* (John 15:1-11).

If you have received this package, then it has been a real pleasure to provide this service. The message was downloaded into my mind/heart like a file from our Father in Heaven, and not from any research efforts. Reading the holy scriptures together with the help and counsel of the Holy Spirit is the best way to learn.

It's now time to KNOW and get ready!
Our Father wants us all saved but will never force us to return to Him.

NB: This message was cross-checked with the Word of God using the New King James Bible from which most scripture references were taken. One reference was taken from the Amplified Bible.

ABOUT THE AUTHOR:

Lorraine was born in London and is a married mother of three children. She holds a BSc in Nutrition and Dietetics, a master's degree in Nutrition, an MBA, and a Certificate of Advanced Studies from universities in the UK and Switzerland. Lorraine works in food research and public health nutrition.

Lorraine gave her life to her heavenly Father when she was 12 years old, and since the baptism of the Holy Spirit, Lorraine has been given different packages to deliver to His earth, and she hopes to deliver them all in due time.

ACKNOWLEDGEMENTS

"I thank You, Father, Lord of heaven and earth, that You have hidden these things from the wise and prudent and have revealed them to babes. (Matthew 11:25).

"Blessing and honor and glory and power Be to Him who sits on the throne, And to the Lamb, forever and ever!" (Revelation 5:13)

Thank you to the most holy and loving heavenly Father and my kind mother, Jeanette, for her loving support and for encouraging me to deliver this package on time.

BEFORE THE HARVEST